BOUNDARIES

After A Pathological
Relationship

ADELYN BIRCH

DEDICATION

To all those ready to fly toward freedom.
Let's soar.

CONTENTS

1 AFTER A PATHOLOGICAL RELATIONSHIP

Life is very different after a pathological relationship. If you have experienced one, you've endured profound anguish, and have gone through profound change. It probably feels as if you need to learn all over again how to deal with others and with life.

If you haven't yet been involved in an abusive relationship, you are likely reading this book to learn how to prevent it from happening. That's wise. Abuse usually begins insidiously and worsens as a relationship progresses.

Abusers gradually wear down their victim's boundaries, and as a result the victim tolerates violations they never would have before.

Abuse includes a wide range of actions and behaviors toward another that undermine their physical or emotional safety. Abusers try to make their partner feel "less than" to diminish their self-worth, in order to gain power and control.

Abuse can take many forms. It always involves a boundary violation, although every boundary violation is not necessarily abuse.

Physical abuse includes acts of violence that cause physical harm or injury.

Sexual abuse includes sexual exploitation or forced participation in sexual activity that is unwanted, unsafe or degrading.

Emotional abuse diminishes self-worth and self-esteem. This is done in two ways. One is through verbal abuse, which includes name-calling, habitual criticism, insulting, yelling and shaming. The other is through the use of underhanded emotional manipulations tactics the victim isn't aware of. It is the covert and intentional infliction of psychological harm.

How can you tell if you're a victim of covert emotional abuse if victims aren't even aware it's going on? There is a list of 19 signs at the end of this chapter that will help you figure it out.

Financial abuse includes controlling access to money, taking a victim's money through theft or deceit, or preventing a victim from earning an income.

Social abuse includes limiting access to friends and family or completely isolating the victim, and preventing a victim from going to school or other outside activities.

Abusers may use intimidation and threats as well. They may threaten to hurt themselves, their victim or the family. They may destroy things, damage personal possessions or harm pets.

Abusers tend to be jealous, possessive, dominant and controlling.

Abuse is often carried out consciously on the part of the abuser, but can also be unintentional due to limitations in the abuser's insight, understanding or ability to behave differently. But that doesn't mean you should accept it or accept excuses for it. Never try to figure out what an abuser's intentions are; all that matters is the presence of the abusive acts themselves and the effects they have on you. You do not have any obligation to be abused by anyone, no matter what their problem is.

According to George Simon, PhD, psychologist and expert in disturbances of personality and character, "Universally, one-time victims of abusive relationships I counseled began to report an increased sense of personal power and validation once they stopped trying to second-guess why the person mistreating them was doing what they were doing and started holding them accountable for the behavior itself. To do so, they had to stop musing about whether the other person did or did not truly intend to hurt them. In the process, they also became aware of how naturally hesitant they were to ascribe malevolent intentions to others and to seek other more palatable explanations for behavior."

If you have been in an abusive relationship, the time comes when you start to look beyond the trauma you experienced. You don't want to let what happened hold you back from living your life anymore. You may even feel ready to take a chance at love again.

At the same time, the thought of dating probably makes you nervous. It's not the carefree thing it used to be. In the past, you never met someone you were interested in and wondered if they might be an abuser. You're wiser now. But you're also wise enough to know that it can be impossible to see the truth about someone in the beginning of a relationship. That thought is unnerving, because you don't want to be victimized again. You wonder what you can do to protect yourself.

After a traumatic relationship ends, it's not unusual to feel vulnerable and need to regroup. You may have withdrawn for a while to figure things out. Now you're feeling ready to venture out into the world again, even though your confidence is still a shaky.

To build your confidence, develop personal boundaries before getting involved in new relationships. Boundaries, combined with your experience and knowledge, can help you avoid becoming involved in another pathological relationship.

A big part of confidence comes from boundaries, because they can make it possible to connect with others while maintaining your safety and your integrity. When you have boundaries, your fear will diminish significantly. You will feel empowered because your boundaries will enable you to communicate your self-worth to others. The more you practice upholding your boundaries, the more respect, love and support you will have in your life.

Boundaries protect your emotional and physical health, and they protect you from the behavior and demands of others. They allow you to confidently express who you are and what you want. Boundaries help you live your life the way you want to live it.

As important as boundaries are, though, they're just one part of preparing yourself for new relationships. Know your weak spots and learn how they can make you vulnerable. Value yourself. Feel your worth. Know what you want from life and from relationships. Learn the facts about psychological manipulation. Learn the warning signs that tell you that you might have an abuser on your hands. Learn how the mind works, and how that makes us vulnerable to abusers and predators. And learn how their minds work, too.

Although boundaries will build your confidence and improve your life and relationships, they will not automatically get rid of the limiting beliefs that caused you to have weak boundaries in the first place. You may need a good counselor to help you identify and challenge those beliefs before you're ready for new relationships.

Become Your Own Protector

There comes a time when you must learn to be your own protector, your own advocate and your own best friend. You may have already been through the trauma of being victimized by an abuser, and you realize changes are needed. The time has come to recognize your wisdom and put it to use in your life. Be willing to learn from your experience and to accept the world as it is, flaws and all. That can give you the knowledge and the clear-eyed view you need to act wisely on your own behalf.

Wanting to make changes doesn't mean there was anything wrong with you before, or that it was your fault you were victimized. It simply acknowledges the fact that there are people in this world who don't have our best interests at heart and who will gladly take advantage of us. That's reality, as we know all too well. The world isn't the way we want it to be — it is the way it is. It's up to us to find a way to deal with that. It's up to us to protect ourselves, as best we can. We are worth protecting. We are the ones who need to have our own best interest at heart.

You learned there are those who deserve your trust and your heart, and those who don't. Boundaries will help you protect yourself from those who don't, without scaring away those who do. They will help you discern who is trustworthy, who respects you, and who offers you a real and meaningful connection.

We all need boundaries, and they aren't just for keeping users, abusers and manipulators away—they're just as useful and necessary in day-to-day dealings with neighbors, parents, siblings, friends, children, bosses and everyone else we have contact with. When you create boundaries you are not building a wall around yourself in response to your trauma. You're simply doing something healthy and necessary.

Everyone needs to have healthy boundaries in all of their relationships. There are certain types of people who need to work extra hard developing and defending their boundaries. We all want to be safe, loved and accepted. But some of us come to the conclusion that the best way to do this is to put aside what we want or feel and allow other people's needs and feelings to take priority. This tactic is known as people-pleasing. This may work for a while. There is less outer conflict, but our inner conflict grows. If we want to say no, we feel guilty; but if we say yes when we don't want to, we feel resentful. It seems we're damned if we do and damned if we don't.

People-pleasers believe assertiveness is harsh, setting limits is rude and requesting that our needs be met is demanding and selfish. Some pleasers don't believe they have any rights at all. They feel guilty for expressing their needs. They consider it selfish to act in their own best interest. Guilt and the fear of abandonment are strong forces in their lives.

Some people believe that martyrdom, self-denial and incessant caretaking are virtues to be practiced to the point of misery. This is known as being a doormat. When people are doormats, they allow others to take advantage of them.

People-pleasers, doormats and others without boundaries don't value their needs, feelings and desires, and put others' needs and feelings first. They feel anxious and guilty asking for what they want or need. They don't believe that they have rights, or don't know what they are (for a list of your basic human rights, please see chapter three). They fear the anger or judgment of others and fear being thought of as self-centered. They're ashamed of showing their feelings or asking for what they want and need. They fear losing love, friendship or approval.

We all have needs, desires, preferences and limits. And we all have innate emotional needs. If these needs aren't met, there can be serious consequences to our psychological health.

Having emotional needs does not mean you are selfish or "needy," it means you're normal.

Our emotional needs include:

The need to be acknowledged.

The need to be accepted.

The need to be listened to.

The need to be understood.

The need to be loved.

The need to be appreciated.

The need to be respected.

The need to be valued.

The need to feel worthy.

The need to be trusted.

The need to feel capable and competent.

The need to feel clear (not confused).

The need to be supported.

The need to be safe, both physically and emotionally.

If you routinely deny your own needs through a lack of boundaries, there is hope. According to Darlene Lancer, JD, MFT, "It's possible to change and find our voice, our power and our passion. It requires getting reacquainted with that Self we've hidden, discovering our feelings and needs, and risking asserting and acting on them. It's a process of raising our sense of self-worth and self-esteem and healing the shame we may not even know that we carry, but it's a worthy adventure of self-reclamation."

A worthy adventure of self-reclamation is exactly what developing boundaries is all about. It's also a courageous one.

But first, an important aside. How can you tell if you're being covertly manipulated in a relationship?

If you are in a relationship and notice any of the following signs, there is a high probability you are being manipulated:

• Your joy at finding love has turned into the fear of losing it. Your feelings have gone from happiness and euphoria to anxiety, sadness and even desperation.

• Your mood depends entirely on the state of the relationship, and you are experiencing extreme highs and lows.

• You're unhappy in the relationship and uncertain about it much of the time, yet you dread losing it because you're blissfully happy every now and then.

• You feel like you're responsible for ruining the best thing that ever happened to you, but you're not sure how.

• Your relationship feels very complex, although you're don't know why. When talking to others about it, you might find yourself saying "It's hard to explain. It's just really complicated."

• You continually obsess about the relationship, analyzing every detail repeatedly in a desperate attempt to "figure it out." You talk about it all the time to anyone who will listen. It doesn't do any good.

• You never feel sure of where you stand with your partner, which leaves you in a perpetual state of uncertainty and anxiety.

• You frequently ask your partner if something is wrong. It really does feel as if something's wrong, but you are not sure what it is.

• You are frequently on the defensive. You feel misunderstood and have the need to explain and defend yourself.

• You seem to have developed a problem with trust, jealousy, insecurity, anger or overreaction, which your partner has pointed out to you on many occasions.

• You feel ongoing anger or resentment for someone.

• You have become a detective. You scour the web for information about your partner, keep a close eye on his or her social media accounts, and feel a need to check their web search history, texts or emails. When they are not at home, you have a desire to verify their whereabouts as you worry about where they really are.

• You feel that you don't truly know how to make your partner happy. You try hard but nothing seems to work, at least not for long. You used to make them very happy and you're not sure what's changed.

• Expressing negative thoughts and emotions feels restricted or even forbidden, so you try to keep those things to yourself. You feel frustrated at being unable to talk about things that are bothering you.

• You don't feel as good about yourself as you did before the relationship. You feel less confident, less secure, less intelligent, less sane, less trusting, less attractive or in some other way "less than" what you were before.

• You always feel you're falling short of your partner's expectations. You feel inadequate.

• You often feel guilty and find yourself apologizing a lot. You continually try to repair damage you believe you've caused. You blame yourself for your partner pulling away from you. You can't understand why you keep sabotaging the relationship.

• You carefully control your words, actions and emotions around your partner to keep him or her from withdrawing their affection again.

• At times, you erupt like an emotional volcano filled with anger, frustration and even hostility. You have never acted this way before and vow that you will stop, but no matter how hard you try it keeps happening.

• You do things you aren't really comfortable with or that go against your values, limits or boundaries, in order to make your partner happy and keep the relationship intact.

You should have your answer.

You might be wondering why you or anyone else would stay in a relationship that causes fear, anxiety, depression, self-doubt, confusion and frustration.

These relationships don't start out this way. In fact, they often get off to an amazing start. He or she may seem like the perfect partner—maybe even a soul mate—and the honeymoon phase is idyllic. When things take a turn for the worse, the victim has no idea what's really going on. Naturally, they try to work things out and regain what was once so promising and wonderful. Having been manipulated into blaming themselves for the problems, they hang on and desperately try to repair the damage they believe they caused and to regain their partner's love. Their loyalty seems to pay off and their partner is once again close and loving... for a while. It becomes a cycle, one they are not aware of. The drama and intensity distract them from the bigger picture.

Second, manipulation begins slowly and insidiously, and gradually escalates. "Manipulation is an evolving process over time," according to Harriet B. Braiker, PhD., author of "Who's Pulling Your Strings." Braiker says victims are controlled through a series of promised gains and threatened losses, covertly executed through a variety of manipulation tactics. In other words, the manipulation builds gradually as the abuser creates uncertainty and doubt by going back and forth from giving you what you desire and threatening to take it away.

Beware of relationships that substitute intensity for emotional intimacy.

Now, back to boundaries!

"Make no mistake—your needs are every bit as important as everyone else's. If you don't believe that, you are unconsciously setting yourself up to be disrespected. Not because you deserve it, but because there are people who will be more than happy to take advantage of you."

2 WHAT ARE BOUNDARIES?

Do you have weak or nonexistent boundaries? Are you unsure of what boundaries are? You're not alone. It's time to learn about boundaries and create your own so you can experience what a difference they can make in your life.

Boundaries protect you and everything you hold dear—your dreams, your goals, your values, your time, your autonomy, your money, your self-worth, your emotional well-being, your physical health, your safety and your self-respect. Boundaries keep you intact. They allow you to live your life the way you want to live it. Boundaries are invisible and are held in place by your decisions and actions.

If you have no boundaries or weak boundaries, the space where they should be is probably filled with things like low self-worth, self-doubt, insecurity, fear of rejection, the need for approval, and a whole lot of disappointment and resentment. These ingredients are a recipe for an unfulfilled life and damaging relationships with users, abusers and manipulators.

So many of us walk around each day with no real sense of our true worth. We may not know what our basic rights are as human beings. We don't know who we should give our trust to. We believe that everyone has our best interests at heart. We believe that other people's needs and desires are more important than our own. We believe that pleasing someone else is worth sacrificing ourselves for, worth giving up our happiness, our desires, our values, our self-respect, and even our most deeply held dreams for ourselves and our lives.

When we don't have boundaries, we neglect who we are and what we want. As a result, we see the skewed image of ourselves reflected in the eyes of those to whom we give our power, and we mistake it for the truth.

I was talking about boundaries with a friend. She said she didn't want to have any of those, because she believed boundaries were barriers that keep people out, preventing close relationships and intimacy. Actually, they are quite the opposite. Boundaries are not barriers...at least not to the kind of people you want to have in your life.

So what exactly are boundaries?

Anne Katherine, M.A., author of *Where To Draw the Line,*

describes boundaries as limits you set to protect the integrity of your day, your energy, your home, your money, your health, your children, your priorities, the health of your relationships and the pursuits of your heart.

If these things are true, why are so many of us afraid of boundaries?

Many of us find it hard to set boundaries and defend them because we fear doing so will cause rejection or abandonment. We may avoid confrontations to make things easier. We may feel guilt if we say no or if we think we might hurt someone's feelings. We fear boundaries will keep us from being loved.

If we're afraid to have boundaries, it means we care more about what others think of us than what we think about ourselves. In doing so we lose respect for ourselves and our self-worth suffers. Others lose respect for us, too.

Having boundaries doesn't mean you're a selfish or unloving person. If anyone tells you that, they are attempting to manipulate you or they are very misguided. According to George Simon, Phd, "Sometimes overly conscientious people equate acting in their own best interest with being 'selfish.' Nothing can be further from the truth. Selfishness is self-absorption, self-seeking behavior that either disregards the rights and needs of others or tramples them deliberately in favor of personal gain. Taking the time and care to tend to your own legitimate wants and needs while not unnecessarily inflicting harm on others (i.e., self-assertion) is perfectly healthy and desirable. That doesn't mean that a good manipulator won't try to convince you that you're somehow doing wrong to take care of yourself. But in your heart, you should know the difference between mistreating someone else and simply taking care of yourself.

If you've had weak boundaries for years, be patient with yourself. It takes time, commitment, courage, and a lot of practice to take a stand for who you are and what you want.

A Word of Warning:

The information in this book is not meant to enable you to "fix" a current or past relationship with a toxic person who abuses or abused you. This book is meant to help you establish new and healthy relationships and help you avoid becoming involved with another abuser.

If you're involved with a dangerous person—one who harms you physically, emotionally, mentally, spiritually, sexually, socially or financially—the only boundaries that will keep you safe are physical boundaries, meaning physical distance between you and that person and no contact at all with them. If you start setting verbal boundaries with a dangerous person, they will see it as a challenge they need to defeat. Consider the risk before taking any action. Physical boundaries and no contact may be your only choice in such a situation.

Anyone who purposefully harms you in any way will not respect your boundaries and they will not respect you. Setting and enforcing boundaries won't help, and may make things worse. The only answer for dealing with these toxic people is to leave the relationship.

"When we don't have boundaries,
we neglect who we are and what we want.
As a result, we see the skewed image of
ourselves reflected in the eyes of those to
whom we give our power, and we
mistake it for the truth."

3 YOU HAVE BASIC HUMAN RIGHTS

Basic human rights are the foundation of our boundaries. All of us have these rights. Unfortunately, they often get trampled or forgotten as we make our way through life. Some of us never knew these rights belonged to us in the first place. This list of basic rights does not include political rights.

Your Basic Human Rights

I have the right to my own needs and feelings and to have them be as important as anyone else's.

I have the right to experience my feelings and to express them, if I want to.

I have the right to not be held responsible for other people's feelings.

I have the right to express my opinions.

I have the right to decide what my priorities are.

I have the right to be independent if I want to.

I have the right to decide how I spend my time.

I have the right to choose how I live my life.

I have the right to change myself, my behaviors, my values, my life situation, and my life.

I have the right to change my mind.

I have the right to make mistakes.

I have the right to develop and express my talents and interests.

I have the right to choose who I spend my time with.

I have the right to choose who I share my body with.

I have the right to be treated with dignity and respect by everyone I come into contact with.

I have the right to be listened to respectfully.

I have the right to ask for what I want.

I have the right to say no.

I have the right to set limits and boundaries.

I have the right to set limits on how I will be treated by others.

I have the right to walk away from relationships that I determine are not good for me.

I have the right to have my boundaries respected.

You also have the right to have these basic human rights, and you have the right to stand up for them.

How did you feel when you read the list? Maybe you felt you were hearing something you'd forgotten. Maybe you felt angry as you were reminded of the ways others had violated these rights. Maybe you felt you were hearing about them for the first time, and you wish you'd known about them long ago. They belong to you, and it's up to you to protect them. They are worth protecting. If you do that, guess what? You've got boundaries.

Keep this list where you'll see it. Read it each day so they will stay fresh in your mind and so you won't forget them again.

4 WHAT ARE SIGNS OF WEAK BOUNDARIES?

When you have weak boundaries, every act of self-denial and compliance eats away at your self-respect and the respect that others have for you. It's ironic that we have weak boundaries because we believe our behavior will gain the love and respect of others. People will certainly take advantage of your willing nature, but their respect for you will diminish, undermining the love you were hoping to gain or maintain.

Signs of Weak Boundaries

Ongoing anger at yourself or someone else.

Feeling resentful.

Low self-worth and self-esteem.

Apologizing frequently.

Doing things that make you uncomfortable.

Doing things you really don't want to do.

Going along with someone else's relationship agenda.

Going against your personal values, rights or needs to please others.

Putting other's needs ahead of your own.

Being sexual when you really don't want to, or engaging in sexual acts that make you uncomfortable.

Letting someone touch you when it makes you uncomfortable.

Not being able to notice when someone else's behavior is inappropriate.

Telling someone intimate details about your life when you've just met them.

Staying in a relationship that makes you unhappy.

Returning to a relationship when you know you shouldn't.

Letting others direct your life.

Giving as much as you can, without getting as much or anything in return.

Allowing someone to take as much as they can from you.

Being overwhelmed and preoccupied with someone.

Accepting food, drinks or gifts that you really don't want.

Committing yourself to something that you don't have the time or desire to do.

Letting others describe your reality (letting others tell you what your thoughts, emotions and motivations are)

Letting others define you.

Not being able to assertively ask for what you want.

Feeling responsible for other people's feelings and problems.

Complaining to others instead of talking to the person who is causing a problem.

Becoming easily overwhelmed emotionally.

Seeking the approval of others.

Inability to separate your self-worth from what you believe others think of you.

Self-consciousness and social anxiety.

Saying yes when you want to say no.

Feeling guilty when you do say no.

Saying no when you want to say yes.

Not speaking up when you have something to say.

Adopting someone else's ideas or beliefs so they will accept you.

Not calling out someone who mistreats you.

Becoming overly involved in someone else's problems.

Not communicating your emotional needs in your closest relationships.

Avoiding difficult conversations because you're afraid of confrontation or of displeasing someone.

Doing things out of a sense of obligation, instead of protecting your energy and time for things you're enthusiastic about.

Spending time with people who drain you or that you don't really like to be around.

Feeling you do a lot for other people, but they don't appreciate it.

Ignoring problems or staying quiet to "keep the peace."

Expecting others to know what you need without telling them.

Inability to be honest.

Understand that having personal boundaries is OK. In fact, boundaries are absolutely necessary for emotional and physical safety, healthy relationships and a happy life. Self-worth comes from honoring who you are and what you want. It comes from living your life as you want it to live it, not from living it the way others want you to.

"You are the one who needs to have your own best interest at heart."

5 BOUNDARIES AND LOVE

When it comes to love, things can get especially tricky.

Strong emotions are involved, along with potent brain chemicals and hormones like dopamine and oxytocin. We meet someone we believe is amazing—a once-in-a-lifetime-love, even—and throw all caution to the wind. It's said that love is blind. But we don't have to be! We can love and see clearly at the same time, if we keep that in mind and put conscious effort into it. It's not easy, but the two do not have to be mutually exclusive. Love doesn't have to make you take leave of your senses, especially if you've been through an abusive relationship before.

How can boundaries help you?

When you have boundaries that are based on knowing what you want and need from a partner and a relationship, you will know when things are going off course. You'll know what you won't tolerate, such as deceit or failure to keep promises. You will have expectations of your partner, such as honesty, respect, loyalty, and emotional and physical safety.

Boundaries protect the things that of value to you. They keep you in alignment with what you have decided you want in life. That means the key to good boundaries is knowing what you want. That sounds basic, but many of us don't have more than a vague idea. Not knowing what you want in a relationship makes you like a jellyfish, a, gelatinous blob that takes the shape of whatever container you're put in. In other words, if you aren't clear on what you want in a relationship, you will conform to the other person's agenda since you don't have one of your own.

It's no secret that psychopaths and other manipulators and abusers target those with weak boundaries—meaning those who don't know what they want, who have a need to please others, or who put the needs of others before their own. Putting others first is considered a virtue, but in truth it backfires. There are plenty of people willing to let you sacrifice yourself on the altar of virtue for their benefit, and to the detriment of yours.

If it's so important to us to please another person, when things aren't going well we only look at ourselves to see what the problem is—we wonder what we're doing wrong, and wonder why we aren't "enough" to keep this person happy. We don't think that *they* may be the problem. We don't think about our own unhappiness and dissatisfaction in the relationship, only theirs. Even if we do, we blame ourselves for it. If we know what we want and don't want from a relationship before getting involved in one, we could say "You know what? I'm not happy in this relationship anymore. It started out great, but things have changed drastically. This is not the kind of relationship I envisioned for myself. It's not good for me, and in fact it's become quite detrimental. I will not be involved in this any longer."

If we're highly empathetic and emotionally sensitive we're at greater risk of becoming involved with a manipulator. When we're more concerned about other people's feelings than our own, we are the perfect prey for manipulators. Why is this? Because we bring enough emotion, love and investment to the relationship to make up for the other person's lack of it. We unconsciously "fill in the blanks" they create. While we do psychological cartwheels trying to keep it together or fix it or figure it out, they just sit back and enjoy the show.

When you don't have boundaries, it means that you will put up with just about anything to be loved. But real love and a healthy relationship never require that you have no boundaries. In fact, they require that you do.

You may question how useful boundaries are in protecting you from a psychopath or other manipulator. This isn't your garden-variety insensitive partner, after all. But what manipulators excel at is crossing weak boundaries, not strong ones. If you enter a relationship clear about what you want and what you will not tolerate, you have set guideposts for yourself that will alert you when things go awry. These guideposts will alert you when you're abandoning your own values and desires to go along with someone else's agenda. If you have strong boundaries, you have a chance at protecting yourself from victimization.

But if you don't respect your own boundaries, no one else will. When you willingly push aside a boundary, ask yourself why. Remember that a boundary stands for something you have determined to be of great importance to you. Remember that you created it to enable you to have a relationship that's healthy and real, with a partner who's healthy and real. Remember that you created it to protect yourself from manipulators, who harm you and waste your precious time. This means that giving up a boundary should raise a Big Red Flag. It's possible that you're being manipulated to do so or that limiting beliefs are at work, causing feelings of guilt or fear of rejection. Stay true to yourself, because boundaries will seldom be a problem for a good person who truly likes and respects you. In addition, knowing that someone respects your boundaries goes a long way in building trust.

Will boundaries really protect you from a psychopath or other manipulator? Quite possibly, because they may decide to move on to an easier target if they're not getting what they want from you. Boundaries give you a fighting chance— maybe your only chance—to prevent entanglement with a manipulator. And if the person is not a manipulator, boundaries give you the ability to create the healthy relationship you want, with a good person you can trust and who respects you.

"Putting others first is considered a virtue, but in truth it backfires. There are plenty of people willing to let you sacrifice yourself on the altar of virtue for their benefit, and to your detriment."

6 KNOW WHAT YOU WANT

It is vital to know what you want from a relationship and a partner before you get involved. A vague idea isn't good enough, and in fact it's downright dangerous. If you don't know what you want, how will you know when you're not getting it?

When we're hoping love will come into our lives, no one thinks "I want to be in an unhappy relationship with a person who is out to dominate, humiliate and use me. Ideally, he'll be someone who has no respect for me and who will manipulate me into losing all respect for myself. He must be able to take control of me so he can hurt me deeply and repeatedly, and yet keep me running back for more with just a few kind words and worn-out promises. I want him to be a liar and I want to be let down in every way. I want to give up all the dreams I ever had for myself in exchange for a few stale crumbs of false affection. I want to be kept in constant turmoil as I wonder where I stand with him, what I'm doing wrong, how I can make him happy, where he really is right now, and what will happen tomorrow. I want someone who will waste my time while he abuses me and diminishes me until I don't have the strength to stand up and walk away. I want to learn to blame myself for all of this. And I want someone who can make me believe this is love."

Even though no one wants this for themselves, it is exactly what happens to many of us. How can this be? People are sucked into these relationships by way of charm and manipulation every day, and they are kept in them for many months or years, even when things went bad long ago.

How does this happen, and what can you do about it? Have a clear picture of what you want, and the determination to walk away if you're not getting it.

It is vital to know what you want before your next relationship begins. This, along with your past experience, will enable you to recognize when you've become involved in something very different from what you expected. You'll have a chance to see it for what it is before your self-worth becomes so damaged that you are willing to stay in a relationship where you have learned to accept poor treatment and not having your needs met.

What are your needs in a relationship? This is something to clearly and explicitly define for yourself. The list of emotional needs in chapter one is a good place to start. Make no mistake that your needs are every bit as important as everyone else's. If you don't believe that, you are unconsciously setting yourself up to be disrespected and treated like a doormat. Not because you deserve it, but because there are people who will be more than happy to take advantage of you.

How can you avoid becoming involved in a damaging relationship? Start by doing some deep thinking and soul-searching about the following things. Write them down as you go to further cement them in your mind and to provide a written reminder you can refer to later, to check up on your relationship and yourself, at regular intervals:

Decide on the details of the healthy, loving relationship you want in your life. Describe the relationship, in detail.

Describe the personality and traits of your partner, in detail. Importantly, describe the ACTIONS this person would take that show you they actually do possess these traits. Then, describe the actions they might take to show you they don't. Decide which traits are non-negotiable. Decide what behaviors you will not tolerate.

Describe how you'll feel in this healthy, loving relationship. List all the ways you want to feel. Then, list all the ways you don't.

Make a list of your needs, emotional and otherwise.

Decide on the pace you would like the relationship to take. You can and should control the pace. Doing so gives you room to breathe. It gives you time to consider what you're thinking and feeling. It gives you time to consider your doubts, if any. It gives you time to learn about a person's character over time and in different situations (which is the only way). Ask yourself how many times you're willing to get together in the first week? The first month? etc. What activities are you willing to give up to spend time with this person, if any? What activities are you not willing to give up? How long will you wait before having sex?

Think about why you're creating boundaries and write those down, too. Your list could include things such as protecting yourself from manipulators, protecting the things you value, finding out a person's true character, maintaining your self-respect, living your life as you choose, and protecting your basic human rights.

Your answers to these questions, along with the list of your basic rights in chapter three, give you the information you need to create your boundaries. Chapter seven and eight will help you do that.

7 CREATE YOUR BOUNDARIES

You are now ready to create your boundaries. Excited? Great! Let's get started.

Before you begin, it's important to know the different types of boundaries so you can consider each of them as you create yours:

Physical boundaries deal with your privacy, personal space, sexuality and body. They determine who may enter your personal space and who may touch you, and under what circumstances.

Mental boundaries give you the freedom to have and express your own thoughts and opinions.

Emotional boundaries give you the freedom to feel and express your emotions, and help you disengage from the harmful and manipulative emotions of others.

Material boundaries determine whether you lend or give things to others, such as your money, car, books or food.

Spiritual boundaries relate to your beliefs and experiences in connection with a higher power.

Now you can start creating your boundaries. Write them down. Make the list as long as you want or need to, and add to it at any time when you think of something new. You won't be able to anticipate all of your boundaries in advance—you will discover more as they are crossed. Pay attention for feelings of discomfort that accompany boundary violations.

For examples and ideas, take a look at the next chapter.

For more help, refer back to the list of your basic human rights in chapter three and the list of emotional needs in chapter one.

By creating your boundaries, you will have accomplished something profoundly important. You've decided to take a stand for yourself and your life, and have come up with a real and practical way to do that. The next time you become involved with someone, you'll be more confident and in control. You'll be much less likely to find yourself going along with whatever happens. You'll also be much more likely to find the kind of partner and relationship you really want.

When you define your boundaries and make a commitment to yourself to honor them, you will know that giving them up for someone—making concessions, bending the rules—is a red flag. It's not something to be done lightly. Anyone who is truly interested in you and who is trustworthy will respect your needs, values and desires, instead of walking away because of them. If someone does walk away, pat yourself on the back, because you've succeeded in weeding out the type of person you didn't want in your life. You protected yourself and what's important to you.

"By creating your boundaries, you have accomplished something profoundly important. You have decided to take a stand for yourself and your life, and have come up with a real and practical way to do that."

8 EXAMPLES OF BOUNDARIES

What follows are examples of boundaries. Feel free to adopt any of them as your own, or adapt them to your needs.

- I will not make excuses for anyone's harmful behavior. I will not let anyone make excuses for their own harmful behavior, either.

- I will take things slow and control the pace a new relationship. I will not see someone more than ___ times per week during the first ___ weeks or ____ months. This will give me the time to evaluate a new person's character, and the space to evaluate my thoughts and feelings about what has occurred during the time I spent with this person.

- When I meet someone new, I will maintain my other relationships and interests.

- I will not become sexually involved with a new interest for a minimum of ___ months so I can avoid creating false feelings of intimacy.

- I will not go against my personal values, rights or needs to please someone else.

- I will not be involved with a person whose words and actions don't align. I will believe actions over words, every time.

- I will not be involved in a relationship with a deceitful person. I will not tolerate deceit in any form.

- I will not lend money to anyone whom I haven't known and trusted for many years.

- Under no circumstances will I be involved with someone who is married or has a partner, or who is unavailable in any other way, including emotionally.

- I will not participate in humiliating, dangerous or illegal sexual acts because I am pressured to by my partner, nor will I continue a relationship with someone who pressures me to do so.

- I will not give my trust to someone who hasn't earned

it. I will only trust someone who proves themselves to be trustworthy, and only for as long as they continue to be worthy of my trust.

- I will not be a part of a relationship where I am not treated with love, care and respect.

- I will not be a part of a relationship where my emotional needs are invalidated.

- I will not be involved with anyone who mistreats people or animals.

- I will not marry or move in with someone before we've been a couple for at least _____ years, no matter how much in love we seem to be.

- I will not give up the following personal goals: _____ (going to school, writing a novel, saving money for a house, etc.) for anyone.

- I will not tolerate abusive behavior of any kind (belittling, humiliation, the silent treatment, yelling, hitting, etc.).

- I will not be involved with anyone who becomes controlling, jealous or possessive.

- When I meet a new love interest, for the first several dates I will take my own car and meet only in public places. I will let someone know where I'm going, who I'm with and when I expect to return.

9 DEFENDING YOUR BOUNDARIES

Congratulations—you have a shiny new set of boundaries. Now, you need to defend them. If you don't, they're useless. This is the scary part for many of us. It scares us because assertiveness is required, and we may have had difficulty with assertiveness in the past.

Assertiveness can be a terrifying prospect for those who have complied, appeased and avoided confrontation at all costs. Our irrational fear of rejection kicks in and silences us.

Here are two simple facts to make it easier:

- Assertiveness is communicating in a direct and honest way. That's all it is.

- Boundaries communicate what is acceptable and unacceptable behavior from others. That's all they are.

If you look at it that way, it should make it less painful to defend your boundaries. With practice—and it will take practice— you will become stronger and more confident, and it won't be painful at all. Abusive relationships are far more painful than being assertive is.

At first, you will probably feel embarrassed, guilty or selfish when you defend a boundary. Do it anyway. Defending your boundaries takes practice and it takes determination. Remind yourself of your right to self-care.

If you fear that defending your boundaries is being controlling, don't worry. There is a difference between being controlling and having boundaries. Controlling people is about telling them what to do. Setting boundaries is about saying what you do or do not want to happen to you. For example, if I told a friend to stop smoking I would be trying to control her. If I asked her to not smoke in my house, I would be setting a boundary. Boundaries aren't made to control other people's behavior. They can't, because other people are not under your control. George Simon, PhD, writes, "...you don't have power over other people's behavior, places, things, and situations. You have power over the decisions you make in response to those things, however, and it is your responsibility to exercise that power in your best interest. Other people don't have power over you, either... They present you with challenges, and you make a decision about how to respond. And if you're of the conviction that when you do or say something you think is right it should necessarily lead to an outcome you desire, you will only become angry, feel helpless and hopeless, and eventually become depressed."

Boundaries can't control other people's behavior; whether or not they agree to respect your boundaries is for them to decide (and what you do about that is up to you to decide). Our boundaries control our own behavior. They help us to live the life we decided we want to live. When we defend our boundaries, we control our own self-sabotaging behaviors, such as taking part in destructive relationships and wasting our time and energy on people and things that don't fulfill us.

When we tell others what our rules are, we can't control the outcome. They have a choice to follow them or not. Then, we have a choice as to what we'll do about it. Remember that if someone does not respect your boundaries, they do not respect you. That might help you make a decision.

To discern if someone truly respects your boundaries, look at their actions, not their words. No matter what someone says, if they truly respect you they will respect your boundaries and change their behavior. If they reject you for communicating your needs and desires, or they don't consider them important, you really aren't losing anything. It means your boundaries are working just as they should.

You have the right—and the duty—to inform others of your boundaries. It's a win-win situation.

Let's look at a simple, hypothetical situation.

You start dating someone new, and after the date he says he'll call you tomorrow. You say OK, but you tell him that you don't want calls after 10 PM (a boundary). He calls you the next night at 10:30, and says he just had to tell you how glad he is to have met you and how excited he is about your next date.

Even though you may consider this a relatively small transgression, it's important to defend your boundary. Small transgressions may lead to progressively larger ones as the other person learns that you aren't able to respect your own boundaries. When someone disregards even relatively small matters, it should act as warning bell. Many manipulators start out by pushing minor boundaries, as a test. There are others who are simply not capable of understanding or responding to other people's needs. Your boundaries are your personal alarm system.

If you didn't speak up in this situation and went along with the phone conversation, chances are you'd feel angry and uncomfortable and wonder how he could be so rude. After all, you told him not to call you after 10 PM.

Instead, to defend your boundary you could say "I'm glad to hear that. But you woke me up, and I told you that I don't want calls after 10 PM. We'll talk another time." If he calls you again after 10 PM, or if he disregards other small boundaries you've set, you have been warned—this person isn't listening to you, does not respect your needs and wishes, and may become worse with time and with more important boundaries.

Adopt a color-code boundary violation system to protect yourself:

Decide which of your boundaries, if violated, belongs in a Code Orange category and which belongs in Code Red.

Code Orange means stop, think, and then proceed with caution after reasserting your boundary with the transgressor, as illustrated in the example above.

Code Red means Abort Mission. There is no second chance for the violation of a boundary in your Code Red category.

And if someone repeatedly violates a Code Orange boundary, or violates several different Code Orange boundaries, it becomes a Code Red situation.

For example, if someone is repeatedly late, makes you wait, and expects you to change your schedule for them, even after you've spoken to them about it and they agreed to be on time, it indicates that you're dealing with a person who expects you to accommodate them and their needs, and who does not respect yours.

If a boundary problem you're having with someone is not an isolated event, it is probably a warning sign about the person's character. A character disorder is not something that can be changed.

Consequences

In some cases, defending a boundary is just the first step. You may also have to create a consequence for violating your boundary, tell the other person about it, and stick to it. Consequences are what will happen if the boundary is crossed again. If you don't stick to your consequences then they mean nothing, along with your boundaries. Consequences are not threats made to control another person; they should only be actions you sincerely intend to take if a boundary is violated.

A Code Red boundary violation would not require you to set consequences. For example, if someone hitting you is in your Code Red category (which is very wise) there would be no second chance, so there would be no need to set a consequence. The relationship would be over.

An example of stating a (Code Orange) boundary violation along with a consequence:

After a conflict with your partner, he gives you the silent treatment for two days. You feel frustrated, disregarded and ignored. When he contacts you again, you talk with him and tell him you won't tolerate the silent treatment, and that you expect open and honest communication instead. He agrees not to do it anymore and agrees to communicate openly.

After another conflict, he gives you the silent treatment again.

You tell him, "You agreed you wouldn't give me the silent treatment any more, but you did it again. We agreed to communicate openly to resolve problems. When you give me the silent treatment, I feel frustrated and hurt. We talked about this, and I feel disregarded because you did it anyway. If you do it again, I will not continue this relationship."

Now, you have stated a consequence.

If you won't tolerate the violation of your boundaries and you are assertive about standing up for them, bullies, manipulators and other unhealthy people will walk the other way because they don't want a challenge—they want a victim.

An important note: Enforcing a boundary does not mean arguing about it or explaining it until you're blue in the face in an attempt to get validation of its worthiness from the transgressor. A boundary is a boundary, and it's yours and yours alone. It does not need anyone's approval.

If someone violates a boundary and you ignore it, or if you fail to realize they've done it, you may feel angry, uncomfortable, misunderstood, frustrated, put upon, victimized, disregarded, taken advantage of, powerless, or in some way bothered. Never ignore these feelings—take the time to figure it out, so you can do better in the future.

Gordon Shippey, PhD, a contributor to the website Counseling Resource, wrote "Boundaries are defined by individuals, by themselves, for themselves. People skilled at manipulation often challenge our right or our ability to set boundaries, in service of their own wants. When dealing with such people, doing your own thinking, on your own, well in advance becomes even more essential. Your boundaries have to satisfy your moral code and support you in meeting your needs, not necessarily theirs. That distinction is exactly what a master manipulator wants you to forget... The key move here is to resist the temptation to rewrite boundaries on the fly... "

Manipulative people will test your boundaries. Don't fall for it. Bruce Tulloch wrote an excellent article titled "Guarding Against Manipulation by Criminal Offenders," meant for people working in corrections. It's applicable to us, too. He says, "When the manipulator pushes, insists, demands or complains, they want to see if you will back down or take a weak conciliatory position... If you lack assertiveness or have trouble saying 'no', the manipulator knows they are on a winner."

Dr. Shippey goes on to say, "Just because you define a boundary, and even declare it, doesn't mean that others will respect it. Just like political boundaries require border guards, fences and walls, personal boundaries require planning out exactly what to do should someone try to violate a boundary... Ultimately, boundaries are only as good as our skills and resolve to define, declare and defend them."

If you've set a boundary and are tempted to bend it for someone, or let them disregard it, think carefully before you do. It's a serious thing to give up something important to you, and it could mean you've become involved with an abuser, one who will chip away at your boundaries one by one as his or her behavior worsens.

Ultimately, boundaries are only as good as our skills and resolve to define, declare and defend them.

"If you won't tolerate the violation
of your boundaries and you are assertive in
standing up for them, manipulators and other
unhealthy people will walk the
other way because they don't want a
challenge—they want a victim."

10 IMPORTANT POINTS AND A WRAP-UP

A reader commented on my website, Psychopaths and Love, saying "It's hard to enforce a boundary when you don't even know it's being violated."

When dealing with covert manipulators, it won't always be obvious that our boundaries are being tested, prodded, pushed and violated with underhanded tactics. What better way is there, after all, to push a boundary aside than to use subtle influence to make someone think it was their own decision?

That's precisely why we need to clearly and explicitly define our boundaries. If you do this, you'll know when one of them has been compromised. Keep in mind that even if you think you're the one who decided to loosen a boundary, it's still a warning sign telling you to stop and take a closer look at what's going on, at what's really behind that decision. You need to stop and ask yourself why you've compromised or given up something you said you valued enough to protect and defend.

Healthy boundaries are commonly defined as "flexible" as opposed to "rigid," and this may be true but you need to first consider if you're becoming "flexible" with the wrong person or without a good reason, or with one of your boundaries that is simply not open to compromise. You need to honestly ask yourself if bending your own rule will lead to less self-respect and if it will compromise your safety or integrity. Ask yourself if you're really at the point in the relationship where you know enough to be certain about the other person's character and motives, and if you conclude you are at that point, then you need to ask yourself what makes you feel that that way. What is that based on? Is it because you're just a good judge of character? You're not, because no one is. Without facts, and without observing a person in over time and in different situations, you can't trust your judgment of anyone's character. Without actions, you can't believe words. Manipulators are experts at impression management. They excel at making themselves seem like good and trustworthy people.

Boundaries are about what we value. They're about what we have decided is important to us. We create them to protect those things. We create them to ensure that we will get what we want and need in life. Because of this, they also protect us from getting what we don't want and they protect us from those who care more about their needs than ours, and who will go about getting those needs filled in any way they can.

A lot of us lost a significant amount of our self-respect from being involved in a pathological relationship. A big part of that came from compromising our needs and values as a result of the manipulation we endured. Suggesting we become clear about our boundaries now is not saying we were at fault. It's about taking what we've experienced, and what we've learned since then, and turning it into something we can actually use in the future to prevent it from happening again.

Nothing is foolproof, but we need to move past the notion that manipulators are omnipotent beings we are powerless against. There is a point in the journey when we believe this is true, but as we learn about what happened and see it clearly, we realize this belief will do nothing to help us move forward and everything to keep us fearful and vulnerable. We need to realize how powerful we really are, and how much we can do to determine our own destinies.

"Ultimately, people have power only over one thing: the execution of their free will," wrote George Simon, PhD.

Believe in yourself. Value yourself as a unique individual who is worthy of love and respect. Practice self-confidence and self-love every day, until it feels natural. Setting and defending your boundaries is an excellent way to do it.

You get to decide how you want to live your life. Find your courage. Love yourself enough to live in an authentic way. Stop caring so much what everybody else thinks of you, and start caring about what YOU think of you. Your life will become much simpler and filled with much more joy.

"Practice self-confidence
and self-love every day, until it feels
natural. Setting and defending
your boundaries is an excellent
way to do it."

ABOUT THE AUTHOR

Adelyn Birch is the creator author of the website, Psychopaths and Love. She was victimized by a psychopath. She reaches out to others who have been victimized, in an effort to share what she's learned and to offer validation, encouragement and support.

Other Books by the Author:

Psychopaths and Love

MORE Psychopaths and Love (A collection of essays to inspire healing and empowerment)

30 Covert Emotional Manipulation Tactics

202 Ways to Spot a Psychopath in Personal Relationships